"For Donalda, Sileas, Alasdair and Donald".

CAFÉ GANDOLFI

COOKBOOK

CAFÉ GANDOLFI

COOKBOOK

Seumas MacInnes

www.cafegandolfi.co.uk

Contents of book © Cafe Gandolfi Ltd.
First published 2009, reprinted 2010, 2013 and 2018 Cafe Gandolfi Ltd.
www.cafegandolfi.co.uk
ISBN978-0-9564050-0-5

ePub:ISBN 978-0-9564050-1-2
Mobipocket:ISBN 978-0-9564050-2-9
PDF:ISBN 978-0-9564050-3-6

Text: Seumas MacInnes
Photography: Stephen Kearney
Design: Jane Darroch Riley
Concept: Roland Main and John Hatfield
Production Assistant: Léa Ferraton-Delouis

Printed by Bell & Bain, Thornliebank, Glasgow

Contents

Deagh bhiadh - Deagh bheannachd

Philosophy

Deagh Bhiadh, Deagh Bheannachd

Well fed, well blessed. The Gaelic proverb displayed on the wall of Café Gandolfi is my aspiration for everyone who eats here. It's simple yet deeply ambitious, an honest proposition that draws on my heritage and one that's steeped in the values of the Hebrides, where good food is one of life's atavistic joys and where eating together strengthens the bonds between family and friends in a way that's now rare, as we increasingly make do with grabbing food on the run, depriving ourselves of the pleasure of valuable, shared moments.

The roots run deep: my whole family back through the mists of time come from Barra. My childhood holidays were long and glorious days spent on that rugged little island hanging at the southernmost point of the Hebridean archipelago, a five-hour journey by boat from the coast of Argyll, sailing far past the isles of Mull and Coll, out into the Atlantic.

Barra retains its best traditions: a place that is Gaelic-speaking and where people still endlessly enthuse about food: fresh and abundant fish and delicately-flavoured lamb which has been raised nibbling on harsh tufts of grass. There's an honest approach to cooking there, one that uses superlative produce to best advantage and it's one that still informs my credo of superb ingredients, simply cooked and served with care.

We sometimes forget, with typical Scottish modesty, what a tremendous culture of good food we possess: whether it's lobster, served grilled with home-made mayonnaise and chips; black pudding from the Isle of Lewis; or a slow-cooked shoulder of lamb that takes infinitely more care to prepare than some more familiar cuts but excites and rewards the palate with deep, intense flavours.

Of course, Glasgow and the Outer Isles – Na h-Eileanan a-Muigh – have enjoyed a long and spirited rapport: I was born and raised as a Glasgow Gael, and in its first 30 years Café Gandolfi, with its Mediterranean name, has comingled the best and most enjoyable elements of European restaurant culture in a relaxed and cosmopolitan way – while remaining resolutely Glaswegian.

Forget the artifice and whimsy of other cities – Glasgow is gregarious and garrulous, imbued with a sense of self-confidence that reminds me of New York. Anthony Bourdain, the global chef-at-large whose home base is at Brasserie Les Halles in New York – and who came to film, cook and eat here at Gandolfi – described Glasgow as "Maybe the most bullshit-free place on earth ... I think I call it the antidote to the rest of the world".

And in the whirl of a busy evening, when I'm caught up in the banter and the jokes and the sheer sense of enjoyment I think I probably agree. There's a unique alchemy about the Gandolfi experience that I revel in – one that's all about enabling and orchestrating a sense of achievement and wellbeing. Actors, artists and musicians know the constant quest for that feeling of occasion and fulfilment and I think the best restaurateurs also have that instinctual desire.

It's about knowing what people's tastes are, being able to smile and greet them by name, welcoming them back when they return to Gandolfi. It's about a multitude of small gestures of kindness – and when I see the same faces year after year with the same smiles of appreciation I find it incredibly rewarding.

Not all choices are freely made: Café Gandolfi chose me as much as I chose it but I wouldn't and I can't have it otherwise. Thirty years after its doors first opened the contented consensus (elicited from a growing global constituency) is that their next visit is eagerly anticipated – and will be, preferably, soon. Well fed, well blessed? I believe they will be.

A slice of life at Café Gandolfi

When I walk into Café Gandolfi every morning at half past eight, with the sun slanting through the big windows, the place is coming alive. Deliveries are arriving: bread, groceries, the fishmonger's van – and everyone is slipping easily into their routine, anticipating the first customers of the day.

Since it opened 30 years ago, Café Gandolfi has woven itself into the fabric of Glasgow's social life. I can't imagine the city without it now and it's an immensely comforting thought that if someone were to walk in here after 30 years, they would find the place immediately familiar, much as they saw it last, which is a huge tribute to its enduring appeal.

The sight of impeccably fresh ingredients being delivered from all over Scotland is still a source of excitement to me. There's meat on a daily basis and a weekly consignment of white and black pudding from Stornoway; cold-smoked, wild venison comes from Rannoch and smoked salmon from Achiltibuie; the oatcakes are from Benbecula and the haggis from Dingwall. There are langoustines sourced from Scottish waters, organic fresh salmon and, in season, asparagus, Scottish strawberries and Ayrshire potatoes.

The doors open at 9am for breakfast. Some people linger to read the newspapers while others in suits open their briefcases and get down to some early business over a coffee. Shoppers drop by for scones and tea and old friends enjoy a chat. Then, from noon, the tempo and the scene changes as new diners arrive for lunch and the hum of conversation gradually rises.

There's an innate friendliness and a homeliness here that makes Gandolfi a comfort zone. These are qualities that have grown organically and ones that I have tried to nurture. It's important that everyone feels comfortable, whether it's ladies coming in for lunch or an evening meal on their own or parents with small babies who know that the staff will make them feel relaxed. They're confident that they'll get the same degree of attention as the great and the good, the politicians, musical celebrities or film stars who appreciate the intimacy and privacy they find here.

And these little slices of life continue into the evening. The door constantly revolves as people come and go, some arriving for a hot chocolate and brandy before going to the cinema, some for an early evening meal and a glass of wine at the bar upstairs while others are relaxing over dinner or celebrating a wedding, birthday party or bar mitzvah.

If good food is a sine qua non, so is good wine – and selecting it here isn't the ordeal that it can become in some restaurants. Customers shouldn't have to agonise about the choice so we take the pressure away and make it easy for them. I offer them what I like: Gandolfi has 34 wines by the glass, from Sancerre and Rioja Blanco through Australian Shiraz and Tuscan Sangiovese to dessert wines and Champagne, all allowing people to experiment, try something new and broaden their taste. Lynne, our manager, has a superb understanding of what wines work best with our food, beginning with the French classics such as Burgundy, Côtes du Rhônes and Beaujolais and taking in an eclectic global selection.

Just as I took over ownership of the restaurant, my parents bought a retirement house in France where we used to bottle wine from barrels. In 2002, when we were celebrating my father's 80th birthday here, we all raised a glass of Champagne to him upstairs – and to the opening of Bar Gandolfi. This gave a new dimension to the restaurant. It's an exciting, elegant, bright space that's different

but still quintessentially Gandolfi, retaining the white ceramic tiles that echo its beginnings in the old cheese market and with furniture from the Tim Stead Workshop, still very familiar but more streamlined.

It's a grown-up bar, probably the only one in Glasgow where it feels completely natural to have a glass of Champagne with your mince and tatties. Like the café, it has a unique authenticity and it works. I have a fierce conviction that it works because I've always been a restaurateur, not an entrepreneur. Café Gandolfi isn't a brand that can easily be replicated or transported elsewhere: its roots are deep in the history and heart of Glasgow and, above all, it's my passion. If you lose the passion you lose the place that gave you that excitement in the first place.

The qualities that turned a new, optimistic venture in the Merchant City into a much-loved institution for diners from Glasgow – and, increasingly, all over the world – aren't negotiable: it's a place for excellent, honestly-prepared Scottish food, for wine and laughter. It's a place for conversation, an intimate place. Somewhere you can step into and feel that you're in your own little bubble.

For me, it isn't a real Gandolfi day if I'm not there – I can hardly bear being away – but nothing would happen without the staff. Anne Marie and Stuart are Gandolfi veterans and have worked five decades at the café between them. If I'm not around they're the ones that people instantly recognise. All the staff know intuitively how I work. If problems arise they deal with them quickly and efficiently and they've been a vital part of the restaurant constantly getting better.

It's also inspiring to have people who share my belief in maintaining a light-hearted atmosphere. We all work very hard to make Café Gandolfi what it is – but a busy restaurant is a high-pressure environment and if we were to take ourselves too seriously, we'd explode. We just keep things running and have a laugh about it later.

We close at midnight and after the goodbyes are said to the last customers of the evening there's still plenty to do – but as the pressure hisses out of the coffee machine it signals a gentle easing off. At that stage I can sit down, take a breath, maybe have a glass of wine, reflect on the day that's passed and think about the next morning at Gandolfi. Because I have no plans to be anywhere else.

The history

In 1979, Glasgow's Merchant City seemed an epoch away from the vibrant, cosmopolitan place it now is. Elegant streets and stylish buildings constructed by the city's 18th and 19th century fathers were neglected, shabby and down-at-heel – not remotely the kind of area likely to attract restaurant-goers. In fact, there were no restaurants.

That was about to change. When Iain Mackenzie, Café Gandolfi's founder, saw the empty offices of the city's old cheese market he had the clear-eyed vision to open an original, trendsetting and stylish café at the very heart of Glasgow.

It was a leap of faith on Iain's part but he was on to a winner. As a photographer, he brought a sophisticated aesthetic both to the interior and to the food. And, of course, its name – Gandolfi – which was inspired by the company founded by Louis Gandolfi that made cameras which have been synonymous with fine photography for 120 years.

Iain brought a pioneering spirit and an authentic European sensibility: Gandolfi introduced Glasgow's first cappuccino machine and gave the city its first taste of real café society. Glasgow needed to change and Gandolfi arrived at the right time.

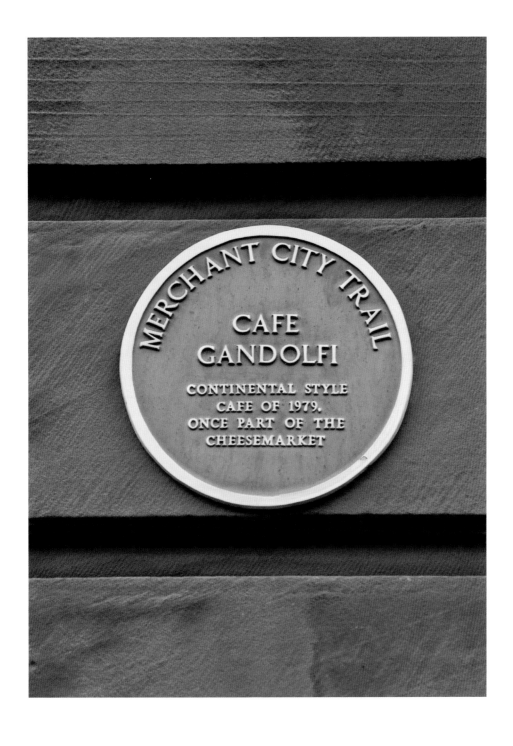

CAFE GANDOLFI MERCHANDISE.

T SHIRTS :— 12.00 OVEN GLOVES :— 10.00 CAPPUCINO CUP:— 10.00
APRONS :— 15.00 T. TOWELS :— 5.00 ESPRESSO CUPS:— 16.00

GANDOLFI SPECIALS

SOUP OF THE DAY :— CARROT, COURGETTE + FENNEL

JULY WINE CLUB.

	BTL	LARGE	REG
SHUTTLEBUTT SAUVIGNON, SEMILLON (AUSTRALIAN) (RIPE MELON & PASSION FRUIT WITH AROMATIC BOQUET)	18.00	6.40	4.50
HAVANA HILLS MERLOT 2005 (SOUTH AFRICAN) (DARK PLUM + DAMSON WITH SPICE & RESTRAINED OAK)	21.00	7.10	5.00

VANILLA AND RASPBERRY CUP CAKE —3.50
* CHOCOLATE + BANANA BREAD + BUTTER PUDDING · 3.95

ARDBEG 10 YR OLD WITH 3 CHEESE PAIRING (ANSTER, ISLE OF MULL & BEAUFORT)
                                                                    10.00

SUNDAY LUNCH AT GANDOLFI FISH
2 COURSES :— 21.00
3 COURSES :— 25.00

PRICE INCLUDES A BLOODY MARY OR A GLASS OF CHAMPAGNE

The admired furniture maker Tim Stead, a graduate of the Glasgow School of Art, was asked to make the sinewy, sculpture-like yet comfortable tables and chairs. With a patina acquired through constant use, the furniture is even more beautiful now than it was 30 years ago. Glass painter John Clark later installed 'A flock of fishes', the two stained glass panels that splash colour on to the big main windows.

When I arrived at Gandolfi in 1983 it was to peel potatoes and chop red cabbage and carrots but as I walked through the door for the first time I was entranced by the big, bright, L–shaped room with its wood panelling, soaring ceiling and marvellous tables and chairs.

At that stage, of course, I couldn't imagine that Gandolfi would ever be mine – but I did know that I wanted a business, a restaurant. By 1995, I'd been a kitchen porter, charge hand, manager and co-owner and when Iain decided to sell his share of the business to me it was like having the flame passed on – I was committed to Gandolfi remaining the same.

Iain and I had deeply shared values: we both have Hebridean antecedents, his in Lewis and mine in Barra. We were two Gaels in Glasgow running a restaurant with an Italian-sounding name committed to serving the very best of Scottish produce, so the formula was unique.

Gandolfi had a warmth, a magic about it, a comfortable, unselfconscious feel. That hasn't changed and continuity is a major part of its allure. People return time and time again, sometimes after a year, two years or more and the restaurant is the same, the heart of the menu is the same and that's the beauty of the place.

I've always believed that the easy part in this business is opening a restaurant. The real challenge is working tirelessly to maintain the standards our customers have come to expect. They appreciate this sense of reassurance and that's why they are so loyal.

Look at today's Merchant City: it's become a high-energy, cultural magnet with dozens of restaurants and an explosion of choice of cuisines. Café Gandolfi can claim to have sparked this renaissance and 30 years later it's still unique. While many have tried to emulate the formula, no one has succeeded.

Starters and light meals

ARBROATH SMOKIES

SERVES 4

2 smokies
1 beef tomato
parmesan cheese
150ml double cream
150ml tomato and basil sauce (see page 118)

Pre-heat the oven to 180°C.

Take the flesh of the smokies and place in a bowl. The fresher they are, the easier this is to do.

Slice the beef tomato and place one slice in each of the ramekins. Now divide the fish and tomato sauce between each dish. Finish off with the cream.

Top with grated parmesan and cook in the oven for 15 minutes and serve with bread and salad.

GRAVADLAX

SERVES 6-8

1.5kg fresh salmon fillet with skin on

500g sugar

500g rock salt

50g crushed black pepper

100g freshly chopped dill

300ml brandy

1 tablespoon horseradish

200ml crème fraîche

Remove small pin bones in the thickest part of the fish with tweezers. Cut the fish in half across the centre. Mix the rest of the ingredients together and rub into one half of the fish. Place the other half on top and wrap tightly with cling film.

Place in a non-reactive container and put weights or heavy cans on top of the fish. Refrigerate for 12 hours then turn the salmon over and leave in the fridge for another 12 hours.

Unwrap the salmon and scrape off the excess marinade. Pat dry with kitchen paper. Slice thinly and serve with rye bread, some crème fraîche and horseradish sauce.

To make the horseradish sauce add a tablespoon of horseradish to the crème fraîche.

BACON AND AVOCADO SALAD

SERVES 4

mixed leaves

2 ripe avocados sliced

bacon lardons

cherry tomatoes cut in half

balsamic vinegar

chopped parsley

Pre-heat the oven to 180°C. Place the bacon on a baking sheet and cook until it starts to colour. Add balsamic vinegar and let it reduce in the hot oven.

Divide the leaves between the plates and add the tomatoes and slices of avocado. Top with the bacon and spoon the remaining liquid over the leaves and garnish with parsley.

CAESAR SALAD

SERVES 4

2 cloves garlic	200ml light olive oil
2 egg yolks	100ml water
2 anchovies	salt and pepper
100ml sherry vinegar	Worcester sauce
40g parmesan cheese – grated	extra 3 tablespoons parmesan to finish

For the dressing, put the garlic, egg yolks, anchovies, vinegar and parmesan cheese into a blender and blitz until smooth and creamy. With the blender still running, trickle the oil into the dressing and watch it thicken. Add the water to thin it down, season and add a splash of Worcester sauce. Refrigerate until needed.

Meanwhile to make croutons, cut 2 slices of white bread into 1cm squares and fry in butter until crisp. Drain on kitchen paper.

To bring the whole dish together wash and separate 2 heads of cos lettuce and place in a bowl. Scatter over the croutons and pour enough dressing to coat the lettuce to your taste. Sprinkle 3 tablespoons of parmesan over the dish and serve. You can add olives, crisp bacon, chicken or even strawberries and avocado.

ROCKET SALAD WITH ROASTED PEARS AND PECORINO

SERVES 4

100g rocket leaves

4 ripe pears

50g butter

120g pecorino cheese

FOR THE BALSAMIC DRESSING

1 shallot finely chopped

1 clove garlic crushed

1/2 teaspoon Dijon mustard

pinch salt

1 tablespoon balsamic vinegar

120ml extra virgin olive oil

Make the dressing first. Put all the ingredients into a screw top jar and shake well.

After that, melt butter in a frying pan and add the pears. These should not be peeled but cut into quarters and cut again into thick slices. Allow them to colour in the pan.

To finish the dish, divide the rocket between 4 plates and drizzle with balsamic dressing. Place the pears on the leaves and scatter over the cheese, which should be shaved into thin slices with a potato peeler.

CHICKPEA DAAL

SERVES 4

1 large onion finely chopped

2 cloves garlic – crushed

1 tablespoon oil

2 cans chickpeas – don't drain

2 tablespoons tomato puree

2 beef tomatoes cut into 6

1 teaspoon cayenne

1 teaspoon turmeric

1 teaspoon dried mint

2 teaspoons coriander

3 teaspoons cumin

2 teaspoons ground ginger

1 teaspoon cinnamon

1 tablespoon sugar

1/2 teaspoon garam masala

100g baby spinach

Sauté onions until soft, add garlic and continue to cook for 5 minutes. Add all the spices, sugar and tomato puree and simmer for a further 5 minutes.

Cut the tomatoes into six and add them and the chickpeas, with their brine, and cook gently for 20 minutes on the stove. Check the seasoning and fold in the baby spinach.

Serve with yoghurt, if desired. An added twist is to squeeze half a lemon over the daal.

GANDOLFI PRAWN COCKTAIL

SERVES 4

400g cooked prawns

leaves of 2 little gem lettuce

2 spring onions

10 tablespoons mayonnaise

2 tablespoons tomato ketchup

4 shakes of Tabasco

1 tablespoon brandy

3 tablespoons Greek yoghurt

juice of 1 lime

freshly ground black pepper

Divide the lettuce leaves between the 4 plates and sprinkle over the white parts of the spring onions, which should be shredded beforehand.

Spoon the prawns on top and mix all the remaining ingredients together in a bowl. Drizzle this mixture over the prawns.

For that touch of 70s retro flair, dust with a little paprika and serve with a wedge of lime.

POTTED PRAWNS

SERVES 6

175g unsalted butter
350g peeled prawns
salt to taste
1 teaspoon cayenne pepper
1 teaspoon ground mace
grate of nutmeg
juice of 1 lemon

Melt the butter in a large frying pan. When it begins to froth add the prawns and stir until heated through.

Throw in a good pinch of salt and add the spices. Grate a teaspoon of nutmeg over the contents and squeeze in the lemon juice. Remove from the heat.

Divide the prawns between 6 ramekins, making sure that each dish gets the same amount of butter. Place in the fridge and allow the butter to set.

Serve at room temperature with crusty bread or melba toast.

You can use brown shrimps or lobster instead of prawns.

GRATIN OF TIGER PRAWNS WITH CHILLI AND CHEESE

SERVES 4

200g raw tiger prawns

2-3 chopped spring onions

2 cloves crushed garlic

1 fresh red chilli

150ml double cream

75g grated gruyere cheese

juice of 1 lime

salt and pepper

Place the prawns in a bowl with the lime juice. At the same time put your grill on to its highest setting.

Divide the garlic, spring onions and chilli, which should be deseeded and finely chopped, into 4 ramekins and then place the drained prawns on top. Season everything and top with the double cream and gruyere cheese.

Put the ramekins on a baking tray and place under the grill for 5 minutes until the prawns are pink and the cheese is golden brown.

Serve with some good quality bread and, perhaps, a salad.

ROASTED ASPARAGUS WITH SAUCE GRIBICHE

SERVES 4

2 bunches asparagus, 8-10 in a bunch

olive oil

salt and pepper

FOR SAUCE GRIBICHE

1 hard boiled egg

250 ml rapeseed oil or a light olive oil

2 tablespoons white wine vinegar

salt and pepper

1 tablespoon capers

1 tablespoon chopped parsley

1 tablespoon chervil

1 tablespoon fresh tarragon

Pre-heat the oven to 180°C. Wash and dry the asparagus, then place on a baking sheet. Season and drizzle with oil. Cook for 15 minutes.

For the sauce, thoroughly mash the yolk of the hard boiled egg in a bowl and gradually add the oil, beating constantly. After it begins to thicken, add the remaining ingredients. Also finely chop the white of the egg you have used and put it in the bowl.

Serve the sauce with the warm roasted asparagus, as a dip or drizzled over it.

COURGETTE, PEA AND FETA FRITTATA

SERVES 6-8

150g frozen peas

250g courgettes

1 onion

4 tablespoons olive oil

6 eggs

2 tablespoons chopped parsley

200g feta cheese

salt and pepper

nutmeg

Heat the oil in a deep 30cm frying pan. Add the finely chopped onion and cook for 10 minutes without colour. Wash and grate the courgettes. Make sure the peas are defrosted and put them into the pan and warm through.

Now add grated courgettes and crumble feta cheese on top.

Pre-heat the grill as you lightly beat the eggs, parsley, a pinch of finely grated nutmeg and seasoning. Pour the mixture into the pan.

Cook over a low heat until almost set, shaking the pan often to stop the frittata sticking.

Finish off under the grill, and leave to cool before serving in wedges.

CHICKEN SOUP WITH OATMEAL

SERVES 4

1 litre chicken stock

50g butter

2 medium onions

3 medium sized leeks

salt and pepper

2 tablespoons pinhead oatmeal

Gently sauté the finely chopped onions in the butter. When they are transparent add the leeks, which have been cleaned and finely shredded, and continue cooking for 15-20 minutes, watching not to colour.

Add chicken stock to the pan and continue cooking for 10 minutes.

Soak the oatmeal in 4 tablespoons of water then add it to the rest of the ingredients and allow it to cook for 20 minutes, stirring from time to time. Garnish with parsley, although my granny always used young nettles. Don't worry, they don't sting.

SWEETCORN COCONUT SOUP

SERVES 6-8

2 fresh red chillies

3 large cloves of garlic

1.5 litres chicken stock

juice of 2 lemons

675g frozen sweetcorn

1 tin coconut milk

300ml pint of water

fresh coriander leaves

salt

Cut the chillies in half along their length. Discard the seeds and stems and cut across in very thin strips. Peel the garlic and slice thinly.

Put 1 litre of chicken stock in a saucepan and put the rest in a smaller pan with the sliced chillies, garlic and lemon juice.

Bring the bigger saucepan to the boil and add 450g of sweetcorn. Boil until it is tender, then remove from the heat.

Bring the other pan to the boil and simmer for 8 minutes. Then pour everything in the large saucepan into a food processor and blitz until it is pureed. Mix this into the larger pan.

Add the remaining sweetcorn and simmer for 5 minutes. Add the tin of coconut milk and simmer for a further 5 minutes.

Roughly chop coriander leaves and throw them in the soup before serving.

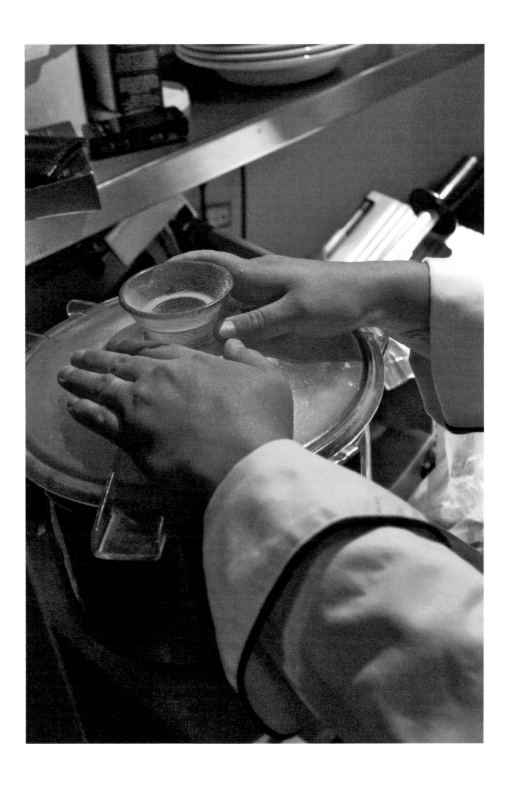

CHILLED BEETROOT WITH POTATOES AND CRÈME FRAÎCHE

Serves 6

700g raw beetroot, trimmed

50g butter

225g peeled and chopped onions

225g peeled and chopped potatoes

6 individual egg-sized potatoes, peeled and cooked

1.3 litres chicken stock

150ml sherry

1 tablespoon redcurrant jelly

Pre-heat oven to 200°C.

Wrap the beetroot in tinfoil and place it in a large roasting tin to cook for 90 minutes. When it is ready allow it to cool. Remove the skin and roughly chop.

Heat the butter in a large heavy-based pan and add onions. Sauté gently for 10 minutes and bring to the boil. Cover and simmer for a further 40 minutes.

Now add the redcurrant jelly and taste for seasoning. The soup should be slightly more salty than usual. Once you have done this, liquidise the whole lot and place in the fridge to chill.

When you are ready to serve, have a hot potato for each person ready on a plate. Place a ladle full of soup in a bowl. Drizzle crème fraîche over the top and place a hot whole potato in the centre of the bowl of chilled soup. The way to eat this is to take a fork and mash the potato gently in to the soup.

CULLEN SKINK

SERVES 4

4 medium potatoes, peeled and diced

300ml double cream

300ml whole milk

250ml water

300g smoked haddock

60g butter

1 onion, finely chopped

1 tablespoon olive oil

pinch of mace or nutmeg

black pepper

In a saucepan large enough to take all the ingredients, sauté the onion in butter and oil until soft.

Add the water to the pan along with the potatoes and simmer for 5 minutes.

Stir in the milk and cream and simmer for a further 5-10 minutes until the potatoes are tender.

Cut the haddock into 2cm squares and drop into the soup. Continue to cook gently for 10 minutes.

Check seasoning and add the mace or nutmeg.

FISH AND MUSSEL SOUP

SERVES 4

900g of fresh mussels	50g butter
300ml white wine	25p plain flour
2 large cloves of garlic	450g skinned thick haddock or any firm white fish
600ml fish or chicken stock	flat-leafed parsley
pinch of saffron strands	juice of 1 lemon
1 teaspoon paprika	cayenne pepper
300ml double cream	salt

Rinse the mussels in cold water, making sure you scrub them and remove beards. Throw away any that do not open when you tap them.

Pour the wine in to a large saucepan and bring to the boil. Throw in the mussels, cover and boil for 2 minutes until they have opened.

Move the mussels to a bowl with a spoon and remove them from their shells, again discarding any that have not opened. However, leave 8-10 unshelled and tip any juice in the bowl back into the saucepan.

Take all the wine and juice in the saucepan and run it through a sieve before transferring it to a clean saucepan.

Peel and finely chop the garlic, than add it to the wine and mussel juices along with the stock, saffron and paprika. Bring this to the boil for about 1 minute then take it off the heat, cover the pan and leave it to sit for 20-25 minutes.

Meanwhile, melt the butter in a heavy-based pan. Remove from the heat and stir in the flour. Put the pan back on the heat and slowly add the stock and cream mixture.

Bring it to the boil, stirring all the time. Let it simmer for 4-5 minutes, again stirring all the time. Remove from the heat, season with salt and pepper and cover the pan.

Before serving slice the fish into 4cm pieces and roughly chop the parsley leaves. Bring the soup to a rolling boil, drop in the fish while stirring all the while. Simmer gently for 4-5 minutes.

Add the shelled mussels and pour in the lemon juice through a strainer. Stir and remove from the heat, tasting for seasoning.

When it is served sprinkle some chopped parsley on top and garnish each bowl with the unshelled mussels.

STORNOWAY BLACK PUDDING WITH MUSHROOMS AND PANCAKES

SERVES 8

Stornoway black pudding,
2 slices per person

200g button mushrooms

2 cloves garlic

1 onion

olive oil

white wine

1 tablespoon sherry vinegar

salt and pepper

PANCAKES:

200g self raising flour

2 eggs, beaten

1 dessert spoon syrup

sugar

140ml milk

50g melted butter

Pre-heat an oven to 190°C.

First sauté a finely chopped onion in olive oil until transparent. Slice the mushrooms, add in with the onion and continue to cook for 5-7minutes. Add half a glass of white wine and the sherry vinegar and allow to cook for a further 5-7 minutes to get all the flavours working together. Season to taste.

For the pancakes, sieve the flour with a good pinch of salt. Add the eggs and the rest of the ingredients, beating until a smooth consistency is achieved.
Heat a non-stick frying pan over a low to medium heat. Once hot, start to make your pancakes, keeping them fresh and warm in a dish towel.

Cut 2 slices of black pudding per person and cook in the oven for 10 minutes, turning after 5 minutes.

Place 2 pancakes on a warm plate, top with black pudding and a tablespoon of the mushrooms.

Sandwiches and things on bread

CRAYFISH AND MAYONNAISE ON WHOLEMEAL TOAST

Serves 2

150g crayfish – cooked or prawns

2 slices of wholemeal toast

2 red peppers – roasted, peeled and chopped

4 tablespoons mayonnaise – homemade or bought

juice of 1 lime

Roast the peppers. Add them, peeled and chopped, into a liquidiser containing the mayonnaise. Squeeze in the juice of a lime and pulse until smooth.

Check seasoning.

Mix with the crayfish and place on top of toast and serve with soft salad leaves.

GRILLED ONION AND SCOTTISH CHEDDAR WITH DIJON ON SOUR DOUGH

Serves 2

4 slices sour dough bread

2 onions

125g mature Scottish cheddar – Dunlop, Arran, Isle of Mull, etc

Dijon mustard

Pre-heat the oven to 180°C and butter the bread with Dijon mustard.

Peel the onions and slice into half moons. Sauté them in 1 tablespoon of olive oil and cook for 20 minutes until transparent and soft.

Divide the onions between 2 slices of bread, place the cheddar on top and finish with the remaining slices of sour dough.

Place in the oven for 15 minutes, or until the cheese has melted.

PAN FRIED SCALLOPS WITH CRÈME FRAÎCHE AND CHILLI JAM ON BAGUETTE

Serves 2

6 medium sized scallops

50g butter

2 heaped tablespoons of crème fraîche

2 teaspoons of chilli jam

1 baguette split

Melt the butter in a frying pan and quickly stir in the scallops. Allow to brown.

Once cooked divide them between 2 sandwiches. Dollop on the crème fraîche and then drizzle over the chilli jam.

PAIN BAGNA

Serves 4

1 long baguette

2 cloves garlic

2 tablespoons olive oil

250g tinned tuna – drained

4 anchovies

1 large beef tomato

2 hard boiled eggs sliced

1 red pepper finely sliced

8 black olives – stoned and roughly chopped

splash of red wine vinegar

Split the baguette in two and open it without separating the two halves.

Remove two-thirds of the dough inside then rub the remaining bread with the garlic and sprinkle on the olive oil.

Make sure the olives are stoned. Roughly chop and place with the remaining ingredients inside the bread. Add a splash of red wine vinegar and close the baguette, leaving it to marinade for at least 60 minutes.

NEW YORK PASTRAMI AND SWISS CHEESE WITH MARINADED MUSHROOMS ON RYE

Serves 2

150g pastrami per person

2 slices of rye bread

1 clove garlic

chopped parsley

1 tablespoon of white wine vinegar

1 tablespoon olive oil

salt and black pepper

100g grated Swiss cheese

75g mushrooms

Pre-heat oven to 180°C.

Place the mushrooms in a bowl with the clove of garlic, chopped parsley, white wine vinegar, olive oil, black pepper and a pinch of salt. Allow to marinade for 2 hours.

When the marinade is ready, place the meat overlapping on to the rye bread and divide out half the mushrooms between them.

Top with the grated Swiss cheese and place in the oven for 15 minutes, or until the pastrami is hot and the cheese has melted. Serve with gherkins and salad, or it can be great with a jar of sauerkraut.

GRILLED LAMB KOFTAS IN PITTA WITH CUCUMBER AND YOGHURT SALAD

Serves 4

500g minced lamb – shoulder or neck fillet

2 tablespoons fresh thyme

1 tablespoon ground chilli

1 tablespoon ground cumin

1/2 tablespoon ground coriander

zest of lemon

salt and pepper

110g chopped cashew nuts

CUCUMBER AND YOGHURT SALAD:

1 cucumber

500ml Greek yoghurt

15 grinds black pepper

1 teaspoon Maldon salt

Simply add all the ingredients together in a bowl until mixed thoroughly.

Soak 4 wooden skewers in water for 30 minutes, then divide up the mixture and shape it around them. If you prefer, you can just roll them into balls and place in a hot oven.

They are great barbequed but that is not possible in the Café so we pre-heat our grill to its highest setting and allow them to brown all over.

Place in pitta bread and have some cucumber and yoghurt salad on the side. For the cucumber and yoghurt salad peel, deseed and dice the cucumber. Add everything else to the bowl.

GANDOLFI BEEF BURGERS

Serves 2-4

450g minced steak
salt and black pepper

This is so simple. After many years of playing around with different additions from eggs and onions to cheese, I have decided that all you need for the perfect burger is good quality minced beef and plenty of seasoning.

Form the steak mix in a bowl with your hands and season to taste. Divide and shape as the notion takes you. This mixture will make two half-pounders or four quarter-pounders.

Place the burgers on a heavy-based frying pan and cook. They need at least 8-10 minutes each side but, after that, it depends on your particular preference.

The add-ons that sit alongside the burger are up to you. For me, it has to be mayonnaise, tomato sauce, onions, gherkins and wedges.

DEVILLED HALLOUMI

Serves 2

250g halloumi

75g plain flour

1 tablespoon cayenne

1 tablespoon turmeric

1 tablespoon salt

1 cup vegetable oil

Heat oil in a deep frying pan and mix the dry ingredients together. Slice the halloumi lengthways into 4 then dip in milk and coat in the flour mix.

Gently drop into the oil, moving the cheese to avoid sticking. Fry until golden and crisp and drain on a paper towel.

I like to eat mine on some rocket with black olives and tomatoes, dressed with lemon juice and good olive oil. Or, put the whole thing into a crusty baguette!

GRILLED HALLOUMI WITH BEETROOT SALAD

Serves 2

250g halloumi

1 packet cooked beetroot

100g cornichons

juice and rind of 1 unwaxed lemon

1 shallot – finely sliced

100g chopped parsley

1 large beef tomato – deseeded and chopped

salt and pepper

Heat up the grill and dice the beetroot and chop the cornichons. Then combine them with the other ingredients as if making a salsa.

Slice the halloumi to your preferred thickness and place it on a slightly oiled tray under the grill until the cheese colours on both sides.

Then simply serve with the beetroot spooned over it and a wedge of lemon.

Mains

CRAB CAKES

SERVES 4

50g celery

50g onion

500g crab meat

50ml mayonnaise

1 heaped tablespoon parsley finely chopped

50g melted butter

Worcester sauce

Tabasco sauce

salt and pepper

fine white bread crumbs

The onion and celery should be finely chopped. Sauté them with a tablespoon of vegetable oil until cooked with no colour. Leave to cool.

Mix the crab meat into the onion mix along with the mayonnaise, parsley, butter, Worcester and Tabasco sauces and seasoning.

Add enough breadcrumbs to allow the crab mixture to hold together then form the mixture into small cakes and shallow fry in hot oil until brown on both sides.

Drain well on kitchen paper and serve with a wedge of lemon.

SPICED LENTILS

SERVES 4-6

400g puy lentils

2 cinnamon sticks

1 large Spanish onion finely chopped

2 sticks of celery finely chopped

4 garlic cloves finely chopped

2 teaspoons cumin seeds

2 teaspoons dried coriander

2 teaspoons smoked paprika

1 teaspoon nutmeg

1 teaspoon cinnamon

1 teaspoon freshly ground black pepper

1 punnet cherry tomatoes

Soak the puy lentils for an hour.

Sweat the onion and celery gently for 5 minutes until soft but uncoloured. Add the garlic, dried spices and cinnamon sticks with a tablespoon of vegetable oil, and lightly fry until the aroma of the spices develops.

Add the drained lentils and bring together. Pour in water until the lentils are just covered and no more then simmer without a lid, slowly replacing water until the lentils are al dente.

We tend not to add fresh herbs but a good handful of coriander would do no harm.

Serve with warm pitta bread, chilli jam and humous, with toasted cashew nuts and crumbly feta tossed on the lentils.

SPANAKOPITA

SERVES 6

4 cloves finely chopped garlic	35g pecorino – grated
1kg washed baby spinach	150g crumbly feta
2 tablespoons olive oil	100g ricotta
2 large red onions sliced	3 egg yolks
1 tablespoon dried oregano	juice of a lemon
1 teaspoon ground nutmeg	50g melted butter
1 tablespoon fresh chopped dill	12 sheets filo pastry

Pre-heat oven to 180°C and lightly sweat the onion and garlic in oil until transparent.

Add nutmeg and a generous ground of black pepper before throwing in the spinach. Slowly turn until the greens are wilted.

Drain and leave to cool in a bowl, adding lemon juice to keep the spinach green.

In another bowl, mix the cheese together with the egg yolks and dill. Fold the cold spinach mix into this bowl.

Brush the base and sides of a lasagne dish with melted butter and line with a sheet of filo, keeping the rest covered with a damp tea towel to prevent it drying out. Brush with butter and cover with another sheet of pastry and repeat with another two sheets.

Spread half of the spinach mix on top of the filo. Place the next 4 sheets of filo on top of this spinach mix and all the final batch of spinach mix on top of that. Place the final sheets on top of this and brush the top with melted butter. Score into squares using a sharp knife. It is best to sprinkle the top with some cold water to stop the pastry from curling.

Bake for 45 minutes, or until golden. Leave to rest for 10 minutes before cutting.

Serve with a drizzle of olive oil and a wedge of lemon, although we find the beetroot salad fabulous.

SWEET POTATO AND BEAN PATTIES

SERVES 4

250g sweet potatoes

1 diced red onion

1 cup chopped coriander

1 tin kidney beans

1 tin cannelinni beans

2 teaspoons chilli jam

salt and pepper

1/3 cup chick pea flour

Pre-heat oven to 180°C. Meanwhile, drain the tinned beans. Squash and bash them in a bowl, but not to a pulp.

Combine with everything else, cover and refrigerate for 30 minutes.

When the mix is easy to handle (if it feels too wet, add a little more flour) shape into balls, and gently press down to form a cake shape.

Pre-heat a frying pan with 2 tablespoons of vegetable oil and seal the patties until crisp on both sides. Place on a lightly oiled baking tray and warm through in the oven.

MORROCAN LAMB

SERVES 6

1.25kg large diced lamb shoulder

6 sliced red onions

6 cloves garlic – finely chopped

100g root ginger – finely chopped

1 tablespoon cumin seed

3 cinnamon sticks

1 tablespoon ground coriander

2 tablespoons smoked paprika

2 tablespoons ground nutmeg

3 tablespoons zahtar

100g chopped dried apricots

100g chopped dried dates

2 aubergines – diced

2 courgettes – diced

2 red peppers – diced

sea salt

Freshly ground black pepper

50g chopped coriander

25g chopped mint

25g chopped flat leaf parsley

1/2 cup toasted pistachios

1/2 cup toasted pine nuts

200g cooked chick peas

In a heavy based pot, fry the red onions in vegetable oil. Do not be afraid of over-cooking the onions because we want them to reduce to a sweet paste.

In a mixing bowl, toss the lamb with a little oil and salt and pepper and begin to heat a 30cm frying pan. When the pan is hot, add some chunks of lamb but be careful not to overcrowd the pan as you will lose heat and steam the meat instead of browning.

To the onion pot, add garlic, ginger and dried spices. You may want to add a little more oil to allow the spices to sizzle. Tip in the chopped vegetables and sweat for 2-3 minutes on a low heat. At this point add the lamb and juice it has been resting in. Cover with water and simmer for 60 minutes with a lid on the pot.

After the hour, add chick peas and fruit and simmer uncovered for a further 30 minutes or until the meat is sufficiently tender. Stir through the chopped herbs and serve in bowls, sprinkling the toasted, crunchy nuts at the very end.

We like to serve this with warm flat bread, or a crash potato or two. (see page 144)

ROAST BUTTERFLIED LEG OF LAMB
WITH GARLIC NEW POTATOES

SERVES 8

1 leg of lamb, about 2.5kg

200ml olive oil

zest of lemon

5 cloves garlic crushed

2 sprigs rosemary chopped finely

4 mashed acnchovies

black peppercorns

2kg small new potatoes, skins on

Start this about 24 hours before you want to eat!

With the leg of lamb, ask your butcher to remove the bones and "butterfly" it.

Put the lamb and everything else into a large plastic bag. Seal it and put it into the fridge. Turn it over 2 or 3 times during the 24 hours to make sure everything is well coated.

Take the lamb out of the fridge an hour before you want to cook it and pre-heat the oven to 200°C. When it is ready, put the lamb in one oven tray and place the potatoes in another.

Roast the lamb for 60 minutes. Remove it from the oven, cover tightly with foil and leave to stand for about 20 minutes.

Meanwhile, put the potatoes in the oven on the top shelf about 10 minutes before you take out the lamb. Continue to roast them for another 20 minutes, so half an hour in total.

Carve the lamb in thick slices and serve with the garlicky potatoes.

ROASTED HAM WITH PEASE PUDDING AND PICCALILLI SAUCE

SERVES 8

2kg piece of gammon ham

2 carrots peeled and cut into chunks

1 onion peeled and thickly sliced

2 bay leaves

1 teaspoon whole black peppercorns

350g yellow split peas

3 tablespoons honey

1 tablespoon Dijon mustard

1 jar good piccalilli

Soak the split peas overnight then drain and tie loosely in a piece of muslin.

Place the ham in a large saucepan and cover it with cold water. Add the onion, carrots, bay leaves peppercorns and the split peas tied in their muslin. Bring slowly to the boil and simmer gently for 150 minutes.

Lift the ham and the split peas from the cooking water, which should then be strained and kept to use for soup.

Place the ham on a board and allow to cool for a few minutes. Cut open the muslin and put the now very soft split peas – pease pudding – into a bowl. Add a good knob of butter and grind over some black pepper and mix well with a fork. Cover and keep warm.

Pre-heat oven to 180°C. Peel off the rind of the ham and score the fat in a diamond design. Mix the mustard and honey and spread over the scored fat. Put the ham in a roasting pan and roast for 30-40 minutes until the fat is brown and caramelised. Remove from the oven and cover loosely with foil for 15 minutes.

While the ham is standing, reheat the pease pudding in a microwave for a couple of minutes. Meanwhile, make the sauce by blitzing the piccalilli in a blender or food processor until it is quite smooth. Then simply serve with the sliced ham and pease pudding.

DUCK BREAST AND SAVOY CABBAGE

SERVES 4

4 duck breasts
100g bacon lardons
1 medium onion finely chopped
1/2 savoy cabbage finely shredded
150g crème fraîche
2 tablespoons olive oil

Pre-heat oven to 180°C.

Bring a pan of water to the boil and blanch the cabbage for about 2 minutes. Drain and immerse in cold water to stop it cooking anymore and to keep it green. Put to one side.

Trim the skin on the duck breasts and season it with salt and pepper. Heat a frying pan (if possible one with a metal handle) and place the duck skin side down and cook for about 4 minutes. The fat will run from the duck and the skin will crisp.

Turn the breasts over and cook for another 1-2 minutes. Put the pan in the oven and roast for 15 minutes. If you don't have a frying pan with a metal handle, put the duck breasts on a metal baking tray.

At this stage, it is important to let the duck rest, covered with foil, for 10 minutes.

Heat the oil in a frying pan and fry the lardons until they are cooked through and just beginning to turn crispy. Remove from the pan with a slotted spoon and drain on kitchen paper.

Add the onions to the bacon-flavoured oil and sauté until soft and beginning to turn brown. Put the drained cabbage in the pan and stir around to heat it through. Then throw in the lardons and the crème fraîche and mix together.

Divide the cabbage between 4 plates, slice the duck and place it on top.

RABBIT AND PUMPKIN STEW

SERVES 4

900g pumpkin

4 cloves garlic

2 teaspoons green peppers, dried or bottled

1 tablespoon olive oil

2 teaspoons caraway seeds

4 fresh rabbit joints

100g butter

3-4 teaspoons Dijon mustard

150ml white wine

150ml soured cream

chopped fresh parsley

salt

Pre-heat oven to 180°C. Peel the pumpkin. Scoop out the seeds and chop the flesh into small pieces. Peel the cloves of garlic and chop them roughly.
Crush the peppercorns.

Heat the olive oil in a cast iron casserole dish over a medium heat, adding the caraway seeds and stirring gently. Add the rabbit and brown on both sides. Add garlic, then stir for 30 seconds before turning off the heat.

Add the butter and, when it has melted in the casserole, put in the pumpkin, green peppercorns, mustard, wine and salt. Stir well. Cover with a tight-fitting lid and cook in the centre of the oven for 75 minutes.

At this point stir the pot to break up the pumpkin into a puree. Cover again and cook for another 20 minutes.

Serve it with sour cream poured over the top and lots of fresh parsley.

PHEASANT CRUMBLE

SERVES 6-8

3 pheasants	200g bacon chopped	**CRUMBLE**
300ml chicken stock	1 large onion chopped	50g medium oatmeal
300ml cider	4 celery sticks chopped	150g plain flour
2 bay leaves	300g mushrooms	50g walnuts chopped
3 sprigs thyme	50g flour	125g butter
50g butter		

Place the pheasants in a large pan with stock, cider, bay leaves and thyme.

Bring slowly to boil then simmer for 45 minutes. Cool then strain the stock.

Remove meat from pheasants and cut into large chunks. Heat butter in large pan and fry the bacon, celery, onion and mushrooms for 7-10 minutes.

Add the flour and cook for a few minutes. Then add stock and simmer for a couple more minutes until the sauce has thickened.

Put in the pheasant and season the whole lot to taste before placing in a gratin dish. Allow to cool (you can do this the day before and leave in the fridge as long as you let it come back to room temperature) before putting the crumble on top.

FOR THE CRUMBLE

Place oats, flour, nuts in a bowl and rub in butter until you have a crumble mix. Stir in walnuts, season and sprinkle over the pheasant.

Bake for 60 minutes at around 160-180°C until golden brown and bubbling.

OXTAIL CASSOULET

SERVES 6

350g dried cannellini or haricot beans

3 large onions

2 tablespoons olive oil

900g-1kg oxtail

450ml dry cider

1 orange

100g pitted prunes

1 large red pepper

3-4 bay leaves

1 teaspoon juniper berries

3 large cloves garlic

400g tin chopped tomatoes

salt and black pepper

Soak the beans in cold water overnight. When you are ready to start the dish, pre-heat the oven to 240°C. Peel and slice the onions.

Heat the olive oil in a large frying pan over a high heat. Add the oxtail and cook until it is brown, turning occasionally.

Remove from the pan and transfer to a large casserole dish with a spatula. In the pan, add the onions and fry until soft and browned. Put the onions in the casserole with the cider and rind and juice of the orange.

Meanwhile, cut the pitted prunes in half and slice the pepper in half along its length to remove its seeds and stem, then slice across thinly.

Add the prunes, pepper, bay leaves and juniper berries to the casserole and stir to mix all the ingredients together. Season with salt and black pepper.

Cover the casserole and cook for about 20 minutes until the liquid is bubbling. Turn the oven down to 140°C and cook for 90 minutes.

As that is going on, drain the beans and put them in a large pan of unsalted water. Boil for 40-60 minutes until they are soft but not yet breaking up. Peel the garlic and slice the cloves across thinly.

After the oxtail has been cooking for 90 minutes add the beans, garlic and tomatoes. Cover it all up again and put back in the oven for 2 1/2 - 3 hours until the meat is falling off the bone.

CHICKEN CACCIATORE

SERVES 4

60ml olive oil

1 large onion finely chopped

3 cloves garlic crushed

1 stalk celery – finely chopped

150g pancetta finely cubed

125g button mushrooms sliced

4 chicken thighs

4 chicken drumsticks

80ml white wine

800g tinned chopped tomatoes

1/2 teaspoon sugar

1 bay leaf

sprinkling of rosemary and oregano

Heat half the oil in a large flame-proof casserole dish and add the onions, garlic and celery. Cook until the onions begin to soften.

Add the pancetta and mushrooms and continue to cook for 10 minutes. Remove from the pan and place on a plate ready to be added later.

Add the remaining oil and brown the chicken pieces. Once browned, place everything in the casserole dish and let it simmer for 30 minutes. If the sauce is too thin, take the lid off and continue for another 5-10 minutes.

STOLEN CHICKEN

SERVES 6

10 or 12 chicken thighs, skin on

15-20 new potatoes skin on

1 lemon

4 cloves garlic peeled and crushed

5 or 6 tablespoons olive oil

salt and ground black pepper

Pre-heat oven to 175°C.

Slash the chicken thighs 2 or 3 times and put them into a large bowl with the potatoes.

Mix together the juice of the lemon, olive oil and crushed garlic and pour over the chicken and potatoes. Mix everything together with your hands, making sure that the oil and lemon mix thoroughly coats everything.

Put the chicken and potatoes in a single layer in a large roasting pan. Scrape over any oil and lemon juice left in the bowl and season well with plenty of salt and pepper. Place the lemon skins in the pan to caramelise and roast with the chicken.

Roast in the oven for 40 minutes, basting once or twice. The chicken and potatoes should be brown and there will be a lovely lemony sauce in the pan to serve with it.

This recipe can be doubled, or even trebled up. It's very well behaved and is a great dish for a crowd.

GARLIC CHICKEN

SERVES 6

1 oven ready chicken, 2kg-2.5kg

2 bulbs garlic broken into unpeeled cloves

1 glass white wine

olive oil

salt and freshly ground black pepper

Pre-heat oven to 120°C and have ready a heavy casserole pot with a well fitting lid.

Rub the chicken with plenty of olive oil and season well. Then place it in the casserole pot and throw over the garlic and pour in the wine.

Cut a piece of foil slightly larger than the casserole pan and place over it. Then put the lid on, as this effectively creates a steam oven.

Put the pan in the pre-heated oven and roast for 75 minutes. At this stage, remove from the oven and lift off the lid and foil. Increase the oven temperature to 180°C and put the chicken back in for another 20 minutes until the skin has browned.

Serve with mash potatoes and squeeze the garlic from its skin to eat with the chicken.

ROASTED CHICKEN WITH SHERRY AND SMOKED PAPRIKA SAUCE

SERVES 4

4 chicken breasts

1 large Spanish onion sliced

4 cloves chopped garlic

200ml chicken stock

100ml dry sherry

100g black olives

200g roasted red peppers (bought is fine)

1 cup chopped parsley

1 teaspoon cumin

1 tablespoon smoked paprika

salt and pepper

1 teaspoon red wine vinegar (optional)

Gently sweat the onions. When they are soft and translucent add the garlic, cumin and paprika and continue to fry until you can smell the spices.

Add peppers, olives, and parsley, and toss in the pan for 1-2 minutes. Add sherry and chicken stock and simmer for 10 minutes.

We use a teaspoon of vinegar to add sharpness to the sauce. If you want to, do it now and leave to simmer for a further minute.

Meanwhile, lightly coat the chicken with olive oil and season with salt and pepper. Roast in an oven pre-heated to 180°C for 15-20 minutes. When you take it out of the oven, pour over the sauce.

MEAT LOAF

SERVES 6

500g minced beef

500g minced lamb

1 onion grated

2 cloves garlic

1 tablespoon tomato ketchup

50g grated parmesan cheese

1 lightly beaten egg

salt and pepper

100g fresh breadcrumbs

Pre-heat oven to 180°C.

Mix all the ingredients together gently with your hands and place in a loaf tin. Bake in the oven for 60-70 minutes.

Allow to stand before draining off the cooking juices, then remove from the loaf tin.

Serve in slices with salad and homemade tomato ketchup. It is always good with potato salad or potato wedges.

BOEUF BOURGUIGNON

SERVES 4

1.5kg beef stewing steak	2 onions chopped
750ml good red wine (Burgundy)	2 carrots chopped
3 cloves of garlic crushed	2 tablespoons plain flour
1 bouquet garni	200g bacon lardons
70g butter	300g shallots
2 tablespoons olive oil	200g button mushrooms

Cut the beef into 4cm cubes and marinate with the garlic, bouquet garni and the wine. Leave overnight, if possible.

Pre-heat the oven to 160°C. Remove the beef from the wine and pat dry. Add the beef and 1 tablespoon of oil to a frying pan and begin to brown the meat in batches.

Place the browned meat in a casserole dish. In the same pan start to sauté the onion and carrots. Allow them all to soften.

Add the wine from the marinade into the pan and let it reach the boil then simmer for 5 minutes. Now place the casserole on the heat and sprinkle over 2 tablespoons of flour, making sure it is well distributed.

Pour the wine on the beef and stir well. Cover the pan, place it in the oven and cook for 2 hours. Heat the remaining oil in a frying pan and cook the shallots and bacon until the shallots are softened but not too brown. This should take 10 minutes.

Add the mushrooms and cook for 2-3 minutes. Place the shallot mixture into the casserole and return it to the oven for 30 minutes, or until the meat is tender. Check the seasoning and serve.

GREEN PEA AND MINT RISOTTO

SERVES 6

1.5 - 2 litres chicken stock or vegetable

50g butter

2 tablespoons olive oil

1 onion finely chopped

400g arborio rice

50g parmesan

1 glass white wine

220g green peas (frozen are fine)

2 tablespoons fresh mint

First make sure your stock has boiled, then keep it warm as you start to make the risotto.

Melt the butter and oil and gently cook the onions until soft. Fold the rice and stir to make sure all the grains are coated. Continue to cook for 2 minutes or so.

Add the wine and within 5 minutes it will have evaporated. Spoon in 2 ladles of stock and keep stirring. When the first batch of stock has been absorbed, add another and repeat the process until all the stock is used, stirring all the time.

After 10 minutes add the peas and continue stirring for another 5 minutes. At this point add the parmesan.

Taste and check that the rice is cooked before scattering over the fresh mint. Then stir once more and serve.

KEDGEREE

SERVES 4

450g smoked haddock

1 medium onion finely chopped

120g butter

2 teaspoons garam masala

1 teaspoon turmeric

350g basmati rice

4 hard boiled eggs, halved and quartered

300ml double cream warmed

salt and black pepper

1 tablespoon chopped parsley

Simmer the haddock in salted water for 15 minutes but be sure not to over-cook.

Drain the fish, but keep the water it cooked in. Remove any skin and bones and flake the fish while it is warm.

Meanwhile, fry the onion gently with butter, garam masala and turmeric until soft.

Cook the rice in the haddock water, then drain and allow to dry out a little to let the steam dissipate.

Add the fish, eggs, onions and parsley to the rice along with the cream. Taste and season as required. Sometimes I add extra butter instead of the cream and make it slightly drier.

ROAST GARLIC AND PEPPERCORN TUNA

SERVES 4-6

600g fresh tuna loin

1 whole bulb garlic

40g green peppercorns

sea salt

2 tablespoons olive oil

In this recipe, think of your tuna as a joint of meat. You want to buy it whole, not in steaks.

Pre-heat oven to 180c.

Roast a bulb of garlic for 20 minutes in tinfoil in the oven. Finely chop the peppercorns, then squeeze the roasted garlic from the cloves into a bowl. Add the peppercorns and olive oil and mix well..

Smear the mix over your tuna, cover and chill for half an hour.

Meanwhile, heat a large frying pan and, as with a joint of meat, seal the peppercorn mix on the fish for 1-2 minutes each side. Set the fish aside and allow to rest.

Cut into 4 generous portions and pan fry as you would any steak, to your preference.

We love to serve this tuna with balsamic roast vegetables and salsa verde, but it is equally great with chips and mayo.

TUNA BURGER

SERVES 4

325g fresh tuna

4 tablespoons mayonnaise

1 tablespoon creamed horseradish

sea salt

freshly ground black pepper

2 tablespoons lemon juice

If your fishmonger has a good deal on tuna, buy a bit extra and try our tuna burger.

Place everything into a food processor and pulse and blitz until everything has combined into a thick paste.

Chill for 30 minutes, shape into burgers and cook as you would a normal burger.

Serve with mayo and ketchup on a bun, or a crunchy salad with some mango salsa.

SKATE WITH BROWN BUTTER

SERVES 4

court bouillon

250ml white wine

1 litre water

1 onion sliced

1 carrot sliced

1 bay leaf

6 black peppercorns

4 250g skate wings skinned

100g butter

1 tablespoon chopped parsley

1 tablespoon capers rinsed and chopped

To make the bouillon, put the wine, onion, carrot, bay leaf and peppercorns into a large frying pan along with 1 litre of water. Bring to the boil and simmer for 20 minutes. Strain and return the bouillon to the pan.

Then put the skate in the pan and pour over the liquid until it is completely covered. Simmer for 8-10 minutes depending on the thickness of the fish. You can tell when they are cooked as the flesh is opaque and flakes when tested with the point of a sharp knife. Lift the fish out, drain and cover to keep warm.

Heat the butter in a frying pan and until it starts turning brown. Remove from the heat and add the parsley and capers. Season with salt and pepper, pour over the fish in the pan and serve.

COULIBIAC OF SALMON AND SMOKED HADDOCK

SERVES 8

olive oil

1 small onion finely chopped

165g long grain rice

300ml fish stock

1 sprig fresh thyme

salt and pepper

150g button mushrooms – washed and sliced

60ml white wine

250ml double cream

1 tablespoon finely cut dill

parsley, if available

1 tablespoon finely cut tarragon

1 egg beaten

2 packs ready rolled puff pastry

4 savoury crepes

6 hard boiled eggs

750g Aberdeen smoked boneless haddock

750g organic salmon skinned and boned

poppy seeds (optional)

Pre-heat oven to 180°C.

Sauté the onion in 1 tablespoon of olive oil. Allow to soften but do not colour.

Add the rice, stock, thyme and bay leaf and a little seasoning, remembering that the stock might be quite salty.

Bring to the boil and then reduce the heat and place a tight fitting lid onto the pot and allow to cook off for 10-12 minutes.

All or most of the stock should be cooked off. If not, drain and cool the rice on a large baking tray.

Meanwhile, fry the mushrooms in a little oil and allow to gently colour and dry out.

Put the cream and rice in a bowl and add the mushrooms along with the fresh dill. Season well.

CONTINUED ON PAGE 110

Take one sheet of pastry out of its packaging and open out. Place two of the crepes in an overlapping configuration in the centre of the pastry.

Spread 1/3 of the rice on top, leaving a border or around 3cm all around. Build up more layers with the sliced egg, a piece of fish and another 1/3 of the rice, followed by the second piece of fish and the remaining egg and rice.

Cover with the remaining crepes, shaping to make a tidy and firm topping.

Brush the edge of the pastry with egg wash and top with the second sheet of ready-to-use pastry. Press the edges together firmly and seal. Brush the top with egg wash and sprinkle with salt and poppy seeds, if desired.

Place in the oven and bake for 40 minutes until the top is well browned.

Making the vegetarian alternative is very easy.

The fish stock is substituted with a vegetable stock and, instead of fish, we use drained tinned plum tomatoes and roasted red peppers that have been skinned and placed between rice layers. I would also suggest adding a layer of steamed spinach on top of the crepes.

No sauce is needed with the fish coulibiac. However, I like some melted butter and lemon juice poured over before serving.

RED TROUT WITH CHICKPEAS AND LIME

SERVES 4

8 trout fillets	5ml ground cumin
60ml extra-virgin olive oil	grated zest and juice of 2 limes
10-15ml paprika	2 400g cans of chick peas, drained
5ml hot chilli powder	300ml fish stock
2.5ml garlic powder	2 ripe tomatoes, peeled and chopped
salt and pepper	30ml chopped fresh coriander
1 red onion	40g butter
1 garlic clove, peeled and crushed	extra virgin oil

Pull out any bones from the trout fillets with tweezers then rinse and pat them dry.

Combine 30ml of the oil with paprika, chilli powder, garlic powder and 2.5ml of salt in a bowl and spread this over the fish. Cover and leave to marinade for 30 minutes.

Heat the remaining 30ml of oil in a frying pan and fry the onion, garlic, cumin and lime zest for 10 minutes. Add the lime juice, chick peas, fish stock and tomatoes. Cover and cook for another 10 minutes.

This will become a rough mixture which you crush lightly with a potato masher to bring together. Stir in the coriander and season with salt and pepper to taste, keeping warm.

Melt butter in a frying pan and pan-fry the trout fillets for 1-2 minutes each side. Allow to rest for a few minutes before serving.

Transfer the chick peas and trout fillets to serving plates and drizzle with extra olive oil.

LEMON & MUSTARD MACKEREL

SERVES 2

2 mackerel

40g butter

1 small onion

75g fresh white breadcrumbs

2 tablespoons mustard seeds

grated zest and juice of 1 lemon

1 tablespoon French mustard

1 egg yolk

salt and pepper

1 tablespoon plain flour

lemon zest

The mackerel needs to be boned with heads removed. Pre-heat the oven to 190°C.

Heat 15g of butter in a frying pan, add a peeled and finely chopped onion and fry until softened. Remove from the heat and stir in breadcrumbs, mustard seeds, lemon zest, mustard and egg yolk. Season with salt and pepper.

Press the breadcrumb mixture into the cavity of the fish. Dust it with flour and place in a greased ovenproof dish. Make deep slashes along the side of each fish.

Pour the lemon juice over the fish and dot the top with the remaining butter. Cook in the oven for about 30 minutes, basting frequently during the cooking process.

We always serve the mackerel garnished with lemon zest.

STUFFED GRILLED HERRING

SERVES 4

4 herrings
1 tablespoon balsamic or white wine vinegar
lemon wedges

FOR THE STUFFING
25g butter
1 onion
25g blanched almonds or pine nuts
125g young spinach leaves
25g medium oatmeal
75g mature cheddar grated
salt and pepper

Best to make the stuffing first. Melt the butter in a frying pan, add the peeled and finely chopped onion and roughly chopped almonds and fry for 3 minutes. Stir in the spinach, with stalks removed, and cook until it is just beginning to wilt.

Remove from the heat and stir in the oatmeal. As the pan cools add the cheese and season to taste.

Score the herrings on each side and drizzle balsamic vinegar in the cavities and over the skins. Spoon the stuffing into the cavities and squeeze the edges together, using cocktail sticks to make sure they stay secure.

Put the fish in a pan that has been lined with foil that has been lightly oiled. Grill under a moderate heat for 15 minutes, turning half way through.

They will look great by now, so no need for fancy serving. Just lemon wedges on the plate and a simple salad will do.

CHILLI BEAN TORTILLA LAYER WITH CREAMED SWEETCORN

SERVES 4

2 onions finely chopped

2 cloves garlic

2 diced red peppers

100g chopped button mushrooms

1-2 teaspoons chilli powder

1 tablespoon ground cumin

1 tablespoon ground cumin

1 tablespoon ground coriander

3 tablespoons tomato puree

2 tins chopped tomatoes

4 tins kidney beans, drained

4 teaspoons grated plain chocolate

FOR THE SWEETCORN LAYER

2 tins sweetcorn

1/2 teaspoon ground cumin

2 tablespoons double cream

50g Swiss cheese grated

2 packs flour tortillas

Pre-heat oven to 180°C.

Sauté the onion in 2 tablespoons of olive oil. When transparent, add the garlic along with red pepper and mushrooms.

Now add the chili, cumin, coriander and tomato puree, continuing to simmer for 10 minutes.

Add the chopped tomatoes and continue simmering for a further 10 minutes. Check for seasoning and add the kidney beans along with the chocolate.

Liquidise the sweetcorn with the cumin and cream. Add the cheese and set the whole lot to one side.

To put it all together you need to start with a gratin or lasagne dish. Put a little of the bean stew in the dish.

Now layer with 4 tortillas, overlapping to cover the bottom of the dish. Place half the chilli bean stew on top and then cover with another 4 tortillas. Add the remaining bean stew on top of that.

Put 2 more tortillas on that and top the dish with creamed sweet corn and place in the oven for 30 minutes to heat through. Serve with a little soured cream and a salsa if you feel like pushing the boat out.

Pasta and sauces

TOMATO AND BASIL SAUCE

2 onions finely chopped

125ml olive oil

2 garlic crushed

2 400g tins tomato

1 tablespoon fresh basil chopped

salt and pepper

1/2 teaspoon sugar

Sauté onions in olive oil for 20 minutes. They should be sweet and starting to colour. Now add the remaining ingredients, except the basil.

Allow the sauce to thicken and all the flavours to come together. Gently simmer for 30-40 minutes until thickened

Add the basil, then puree with a hand blender or a liquidiser.

GANDOLFI MAC AND CHEESE

SERVES 4

225g short macaroni

900ml milk

75g butter

75g plain flour

225g grated mature cheddar

1 tablespoon grainy mustard

75g fresh breadcrumbs

50g parmesan cheese

Pre-heat oven to 180°C. At the same time, boil a large pan of salted water and cook the macaroni until al dente. Drain and stir through a tablespoon of olive oil to stop the macaroni sticking together.

Put the milk, butter and flour in a blender and blitz for 30 seconds. Pour into a saucepan and bring to the boil, stirring all the time.

As the sauce thickens, turn down the heat and let it simmer gently for 2-3 minutes, still stirring. Add the cheese and stir until the cheese has melted into the sauce.

Remove from the heat and stir in the mustard. Pour the sauce over the macaroni. Mix together and place in an ovenproof dish. Top with the breadcrumbs and parmesan and bake for 20-25 minutes in the oven.

PESTO

200g basil
4 cloves garlic – crushed
80g pine nuts – toasted
370ml olive oil
100g grated parmesan

Put the basil, crushed garlic, toasted pine nuts and parmesan in a food processor. With the motor running slowly, pour in the olive oil.

There are lots of variations to this basic recipe. You can use rocket instead of basil, walnuts instead of pine nuts. You might want to swap the parmesan for a mix of rocket, watercress and basil with almonds and pecorino cheese.

Whatever you use, the basic method is the same.

PASTA WITH PEPPER AND PINE NUT SAUCE

Serves 4

350-400g linguine or spaghetti

4 red peppers

1 onion

2 finely chopped bulbs garlic

100g toasted pinenuts

2 tablespoons olive oil

1 teaspoon smoked paprika

150g gorgonzola

50ml double cream

chopped parsely

splash of white wine

Wash and deseed the peppers and slice thinly. Heat a heavy-based frying pan and add peppers. Thinly slice an onion into half moons and add to the peppers.

Gently fry these until they are soft but not coloured. Add garlic and smoked paprika.

Cook for a minute then add the cream, white wine and cheese. Reduce for 2-3 minutes over a low heat. Add to the pasta and serve.

PUTTENESCA

Serves 4

350-400g linguine or spaghetti

8 canned anchovies in oil

200g pitted black olives

2 tablespoons capers

1 red chilli

3 tablespoons olive oil

2 large cloves garlic crushed

250g cherry tomatoes halved

handful of basil – shredded

This is all about the preparation. Drain and finely chop the anchovies. Quarter and chop the olives. Deseed and finely chop the chilli.

Heat olive oil in a frying pan and add garlic. After a couple of seconds put in all the other ingredients and cook for 5-7 minutes.

Add to the pasta and enjoy. Yes or no to parmesan? It is just up to you but purists say no!

CRAB LINGUINE WITH CHILLI, LIME AND CORIANDER

Serves 4

350-400g linguine

100ml olive oil

1 medium hot red chilli

1 garlic clove crushed

juice of 1 lime

250g cherry tomatoes halved

225g freshly cooked white crab meat

2 tablespoons chopped coriander

Put the olive oil, the chilli (which has been deseeded and finely chopped), halved cherry tomatoes and garlic into a frying pan and allow it to sizzle for 1 minute.

While this is happening, cook the pasta and, of course, make sure that it is al dente before you drain it and set to one side.

Add the linguine to the frying pan along with the crab, the lime juice and coriander.

Warm through, season and serve.

LINGUINE WITH PUMPKIN SEED & MINT SAUCE

Serves 4

350-400g linguine

250g pumpkin flesh cut into 1cm cubes

4 tablespoons olive oil

100g feta cheese, crumbled

salt

freshly ground black pepper

shavings of parmesan cheese

PUMPKIN SEED MINT SAUCE

150g pumpkin seeds

50g mint leaves

3 garlic cloves, chopped

pinch of ground cumin

1/2 teaspoon dried chilli flakes

150ml virgin olive oil

Pre-hear an oven to 180°C.

For the pumpkin seed and mint sauce, spread the seeds out on a baking sheet and roast in the oven for 10 minutes until they start to give off a pleasant aroma.

Cook and place them in a food processor with mint, garlic, cumin and chilli flakes. Blitz to a fine paste and, with the motor still running, slowly pour in the olive oil. This should be just enough to give it a smooth, slightly runny texture. Season and set aside for later.

Place the pumpkin on a baking sheet, toss with olive oil and salt and pepper and bake for 10-15 minutes until it is tender and lightly browned. At the same time, cook the pasta in a large pan of boiling salted water until al dente.

Drain the pasta, toss it with the sauce and season to taste. Put the roasted pumpkin and feta cheese on top and sprinkle over some parmesan shavings.

PASTA, BROCCOLI, WALNUT & BACON

Serves 4

350-400g penne
675g calabrese broccoli
2 large cloves garlic
225g rindless smoked streaky bacon
2 tablespoons extra virgin olive oil
75g walnuts
parmesan cheese
salt and black pepper

Break the broccoli up, discarding any thick stalks. Cut the remainder into small pieces. Steam or boil it for 3-6 minutes until tender and bright green. Rinse in cold water and leave to one side.

Peel and finely chop the garlic. Slice the bacon into small pieces while bringing a large pan of salted water to the boil. Put olive oil in a heavy-based saucepan and crisp the bacon pieces. Add the chopped garlic and remove from the heat.

Cook the pasta and, when it is ready, put the saucepan with the bacon back over the heat. Add broccoli and walnuts and stir for 2-3 minutes. Season with salt and black pepper.

Add the pasta and serve with parmesan.

PASTA WITH BLACK OLIVE AND WALNUT SAUCE

Serves 4

350-400g linguine or spaghetti

250g pitted black olives

2 cloves garlic crushed

75g parmesan cheese

125g walnuts

125ml olive oil

2 tablespoons parsley chopped

salt and pepper

Simply place all the ingredients into a liquidiser and pulse until roughly chopped.

When ready to serve, have your pasta ready al dente but keep a ladle full of the pasta cooking water to add a little at a time if you feel the sauce is too thick.

Quite often I serve this as a starter, in which case it would serve 8.

Sides

MAYONNAISE

2 egg yolks – organic or free range

1 level teaspoon salt

1/2 teaspoon Dijon mustard

2 teaspoons white wine vinegar

185ml rapeseed oil

Mix the egg yolks, mustard, salt and vinegar in a food processor for 10 seconds. With the motor running add the oil in a slow, steady stream.

If you feel it's too thick, thin with a little warm water.

AIOLI

4-6 cloves garlic

2 egg yolks

1 level teaspoon salt

1 teaspoon Dijon mustard

2 teaspoons white wine vinegar

185ml rapeseed oil

Crush the cloves of garlic. Mix them with the egg yolks, mustard, salt and vinegar in a food processor for 10 seconds.

With the motor running add the oil in a slow, steady stream.

If you feel it's too thick, thin with a little warm water.

CHILLI JAM

1 onion finely chopped

6 cloves garlic – peeled

8 dried long red chillies – chopped

3 tablespoons lime juice

90g grated palm sugar (granulated will do if palm is unavailable)

Fry the onions in oil until they are soft. Then put them in a food processor along with all the other ingredients and puree.

Transfer the mixture to a saucepan and bring to the boil. Simmer until the sauce is thick.

SALSA VERDE

4 anchovy fillets

1 tablespoon capers

2 cloves or garlic crushed

4 large gherkins

3 tablespoons chopped parsley

2 tablespoons chopped basil

2 tablespoons chopped mint

juice of 1/2 a lemon

60ml extra virgin olive oil

1 teaspoon Dijon mustard

salt and black pepper

Put all the ingredients into a food processor and pulse until they come together. It is important not to over-process it.

Check for seasoning, although the flavour will develop as it stands.

HOMEMADE TOMATO KETCHUP

2 carrots

1 onion

250g chopped mushrooms

2 sticks celery

1 tablespoon fresh ginger

2 tablespoons garlic

2 teaspoons dried cumin

2 teaspoons dried coriander

1 teaspoon dried oregano

2 teaspoons smoked paprika

1 teaspoon cayenne

2 tubes tomato puree

l litre water

125g sugar

125ml sherry vinegar

salt and pepper

Sweat the vegetables in a tablespoon of oil until they are soft. Then add everything else and bring to the boil.

Simmer for 30 minutes. Blitz and run through a sieve if you want it really smooth. Check seasoning and serve.

ROASTED CHERRY TOMATOES WITH OLIVE OIL AND BASIL

270g cherry tomatoes

2 tablespoons olive oil

2 tablespoons balsamic vinegar

salt and black pepper

fresh basil

Pre-heat the oven to 180°C. Put the tomatoes in a small oven-proof dish and pour over the olive oil. Season with salt and pepper and bake in the oven for 20-30 minutes.

Remove from the oven and splash the balsamic vinegar over the dish. Scatter the basil leaves over the tomatoes.

MANGO, CHILLI AND CUCUMBER SALSA

2 mangoes	40g fresh coriander
1 cucumber	sea salt
2 small red chillies	freshly ground black pepper
juice of 2 limes	

Peel and chop the mangoes. Cut the cucumber in half lengthways, and remove the middle with a teaspoon, then dice. Deseed the chillies and slice.

Chop the coriander and combine all the ingredients together in a bowl. You can add a pinch of smoked paprika as you serve.

TZATZIKI

1 cucumber	3 tablespoons finely chopped mint
400g Greek yoghurt	1 tablespoon lemon juice
4 crushed garlic cloves	

Cut the cucumber in half lengthways. Scoop out the seeds with a teaspoon and discard them.

Grate the cucumber (skin too) into a small colander or sieve and sprinkle with a little salt.

Stand the sieve over a bowl and leave for 20 minutes.

Combine the yoghurt, garlic, mint and lemon juice in a bowl.

Rinse the cucumber under cold water and slowly squeeze out the excess liquid.

Add the cucumber to the yoghurt mix and season. Garnish with mint.

HUMOUS

300g cooked chick peas (tinned is fine)

4 cloves garlic

3 tablespoons olive oil

9 tablespoons tahini

juice of 3 lemons

3-5 tablespoons Greek yoghurt

1 teaspoon cumin

flat leaf parsley

1 tablespoon salt

It is always better to cook your own pulses from dry, but tinned can be used for a fast food option.

Leave the chick peas to soak in cold water for 24 hours. Then rinse, drain and cook them in a pot until tender with a whole peeled onion, 2 bay leaves and 3 cloves of unpeeled garlic.

Keep a mug of cooking liquid aside, as you will need it later.

Put the chick peas, tahini, garlic, salt and 100ml of the cooking liquid into a food processor and blitz until pureed, adding more liquid as required. If using tinned chick peas just add 100ml of water.

When you are satisfied with the consistency, add half the lemon juice and the cumin before blitzing again. Check the taste at this stage, adding more lemon juice if required.

To serve, place in a bowl and garnish with chopped flat leaf parsley and a generous glug of olive oil.

We often add cooked beetroot, steamed peas or roasted peppers, depending on what we are serving it with. Toasted seeds and nuts can add texture and really lift the dish.

GRATIN DAUPHINOIS

Serves 6

900g potatoes
2 large leeks
300ml double cream
150ml milk
175g gruyere cheese grated
50g butter
salt and black pepper

Before you prepare the dish, liberally butter a gratin dish and pre-heat the oven to 180°C.

Peel and thinly slice the potatoes, which is actually best done in a food processor. Clean the leeks and finely shred them.

Start with a layer of potatoes in overlapping rows on the bottom of the dish. Season well with salt and pepper before scattering on some of the leeks and gruyere cheese.

Continue the process, building up layers and ending with potatoes and cheese on the top.

Mix the cream with the milk and pour over the potatoes. Place in the middle of the oven and bake for 60-90 minutes, or until potatoes are tender. If it starts to brown too much, cover with foil.

PARSNIP AND POTATO GRATIN

Serves 6

675g potatoes
450g parsnips
300ml double cream
150ml milk
175g gruyere cheese – grated
50g butter
salt and black pepper

Pre-heat the oven to 180°C and liberally butter a gratin dish. Then peel and thinly slice the potatoes, which is best done in a food processor. Clean the parsnips and finely slice them.

Start with a layer of potatoes in overlapping rows on the bottom of the dish. Season well with salt and pepper before scattering on some of the parsnips and gruyere cheese.

Continue the process, building up layers and ending with potatoes and cheese on the top.

Mix the cream with the milk and pour over the potatoes. Place in the middle of the oven and bake for 60-90 minutes, or until potatoes are tender. If it starts to brown too much, cover with foil.

HEBRIDEAN BOULANGERIE POTATOES

Serves 6

900g potatoes
1 large onion peeled and sliced into half moons
150ml chicken or vegetable stock
2 thick slices of Stornoway black pudding

Heat the oven to 180°C and liberally butter a shallow gratin dish. Peel and thinly slice the potatoes.

Start with a layer of onions and crumble a slice of the black pudding over them. Repeat the process, building up layer by layer and making sure to finish with a layer of potatoes.

Season as you go, then pour over the stock. Bake for 60 minutes.

CRASH POTATOES

Serves 4

4 medium sized potatoes
4 tablespoons olive oil
coarse sea salt
black pepper

Preheat the oven to 180°C. Meanwhile, par boil the potatoes in their skins for approximately 15 minutes. Drain and allow them to cool a little.

When the potatoes are still quite hot, place them on a baking sheet. Position a masher on the top of one of them and begin to press down slowly. Allow the potato to split, but not to fall apart.

Do the same with the remaining potatoes then pour a tablespoon of oil over each of them and season well with salt and pepper.

Bake for 30 minutes until golden and crisp. Then they become a cross between a baked and roast potato.

JANSSONS TEMPTATION

Serves 8

50g butter

2 onions peeled and finely chopped

2 tins anchovies

8 large potatoes

white pepper

400ml double cream

2-3 tablespoons white breadcrumbs

Preheat the oven to 190°C and grease a shallow gratin dish with 25g of the butter.

Cover the bottom of the dish with the onions, which should be peeled and finely chopped, and scatter the anchovies on top. Snip them with scissors straight from the can and pour the oil from one of the cans over them.

Peel and cut the potatoes into finger-sized chips. Cover the anchovies with them and add pepper and a little salt. Press down well.

Pour over the cream, sprinkle with breadcrumbs and dot the surface with the remaining butter.

Bake for about 60 minutes until the potatoes are cooked and the breadcrumbs are nicely browned.

SKIRLIE POTATOES

Serves 4

1kg floury potatoes
50g butter
1 onion finely chopped
150g medium oatmeal
salt and pepper
2 tablespoons chopped parsley

Boil the potatoes and mash them, but don't add any butter or milk.

Melt the butter in a pan and gently cook the onion until it begins to brown. Stir in the oatmeal and cook for 2-3 minutes. Season and stir in the parsley.

Stir the onion and oatmeal (skirlie) into the mash and shape into a cake. Brush the cakes with a little melted butter bake in a hot oven for 15 minutes until brown and heated through.

They are brilliant served with salmon or lamb but can be just as good on their own with some stir-fried savoy cabbage. They are even more amazing served with a fried egg on the top.

Desserts

CLEMENTINE AND CHOCOLATE TORTE

Makes 12 slices

TORTE:

375g clementine pulp

225g caster sugar

225g ground almonds

6 large eggs

1 teaspoon baking powder

CHOCOLATE GLAZE:

225g chocolate 70% cocoa

175g unsalted butter

40g golden syrup

20g water

Pre-heat the oven to 175-180°C and grease a 27cm pan well by lining the base with silicone/baking parchment paper.

Put everything into a bowl and stir well. Then, pour or scrape the mixture into the pan and bake for about 35 minutes. The top should be golden brown and will spring back when pressed.

Leave to cool in the tin then run a thin knife around the edge of the cake and turn it out. I find it easier to cover the top of the cake with cling film before turning out as it is quite sticky.

To make the clementine pulp, you will need about 450g of fresh clementines. Put the fruit in a pan, leave the skins on and cover with cold water. Bring to the boil, then turn down to a very gentle simmer and cook with the lid on for 60-75 minutes. Drain into a colander and allow to cool.

Split open the fruit with your hands and pick out any pips. Blitz in a food processor to a puree. Weigh out into 375g amounts and freeze in ziplock plastic bags.

Cover with chocolate glaze. To make the glaze, put all the ingredients into a plastic bowl and microwave on medium for 2 minutes. Stir well until it is very glossy and quite fluid.

Leave to cool to 30°C before pouring about half over the top of the cake. Spread with a palette knife. The rest of the glaze can be kept in the fridge and remelted in the microwave or just eaten whole with a spoon.

Sometimes we serve the cake unglazed and dredged with icing sugar.

CHOCOLATE FONDANT CAKE

Makes 12 slices

200g chocolate broken into pieces – preferable 70% cocoa

200g salted butter

250g caster sugar

5 eggs

40g ground almonds

Grease and line a 23cm (deep) sandwich pan while preheating the oven to 175°C.

Put chocolate, butter and sugar into a plastic bowl and microwave on medium for 3 minutes. Stir until well mixed.

Beat or stir in eggs one at a time, then stir in ground almonds.

Scrape batter into pan and bake for 25 minutes. The centre should still be wobbly at this stage but it will firm up as it cools. Leave in the pan to lose the heat before turning out.

You can heat slices of it in a microwave for a few seconds and it is divine with ice cream or with some fresh raspberries.

TRIO OF CHOCOLATE POTS

10-12 Small Pots / 8 Larger Cups

350g white or milk chocolate broken into pieces
120g hot water (just boiled)
150g whipping cream
350g double cream

Pour hot water that has just been boiled on to chocolate and stir until chocolate melts and is smooth. If it is still a bit lumpy, pop it in the microwave on low for 1 minute and then stir again.

Stir whipping and double cream together in a large bowl. Whip the cream until it is quite foamy but not thick. I use a hand-held electric whisk because it is easier to control.

Once you have finished whisking you should be able to tip the bowl and the cream will still move around easily.

Pour the cream on to the melted chocolate and fold in until everything is amalgamated – but *don't* put the chocolate on the cream.

Pour into glasses or espresso cups and chill for 3 or 4 hours, or overnight.

If you want to use 70% cocoa chocolate reduce the amount to 300g.

Variations:

MALTESERS AND MILK CHOCOLATE

Remove the milk chocolate pots from the fridge after 2 or 3 hours and place 3 or 4 Maltesers on top, pressing them down gently until half buried.

MILK CHOCOLATE CAPPUCCINO

When pouring the hot water on the chocolate add 2 teaspoons of instant espresso powder.

WHITE CHOCOLATE AND RASPBERRY

Naturally, this variation uses white chocolate. Instead of pouring in 120g of hot tap water, mix 40g of raspberry liquer with 80g of hot water and put 4 or 5 fresh or frozen raspberries in the bottom of glass or cup.

You will definitely need to microwave on low for 1-2 minutes to ensure the chocolate melts completely.

BAKED CHOCOLATE FUDGE

Makes 12-14 slices

400g dark chocolate (53 - 60% cocoa)

120g unsalted butter

200g soft brown sugar

125ml double cream

2 teaspoons instant espresso powder

5 eggs – beaten in a jug

2 tablespoons plain flour

Pre-heat the oven to 140°-150°C-

Place the chocolate, butter, sugar, cream and coffee in a saucepan and melt over a gentle heat, stirring until the mixture is melted and smooth.

Remove the pan from the heat and slowly stir in the eggs using a wire whisk.

Put the flour in a sieve and sift over the mixture, stirring it in with the whisk. Pour into a greased and lined 28x10cm loaf tin. In turn, place this on a larger roasting or baking tray and pour in boiling water to come halfway up the sides.

Bake for about 45 minutes. It will be quite firm and glossy on the top and will firm up even more as it cools.

Cut into very thin slices to serve. This dessert needs nothing more than crème fraîche or vanilla ice cream to accompany it. Serves many or a guilty few.

DELUXE CHOCOLATE BROWNIES

Makes 12-14 brownies

170g chocolate broken into pieces – 70% cocoa

170g butter

375g caster sugar

1 teaspoon vanilla extract

3 eggs

110g plain flour

65g pecan nuts – roughly chopped - optional

The best brownies are crispy and dry on the top and gooey inside but this method of achieving that flies in the face of convention.

Pre-heat the oven to 160°C. Melt the chocolate and butter in a medium microwave then stir well. The mixture should feel quite hot if you dip your finger in it.

Stir in the sugar, vanilla and a pinch of salt. Beat the eggs and pour them in a steady stream into the mixture. Stir well.

Sieve over the flour and beat well until the mixture is smooth and glossy and is starting to leave the edge of the bowl. Stir in the nuts and pour or scrape the batter into a greased and lined 20x30cm baking tin.

Bake in the oven for 20-25 minutes. The brownies will start to pull away from the edge of the pan and the top will look crispy and dry.

Remove from the oven and stand on a rack to let them cool. This also helps keep the inside gooey.

Cut into squares when completely cold. You can dust them with icing sugar or drizzle them with melted chocolate. Either way, they will be delicious.

CHOCOLATE AND RASBERRY GATEAU

Makes 12-14 slices

400g butter

300g double cream

400g chocolate, 70% cocoa broken into pieces

20-30 frozen raspberries

165g caster sugar

7 eggs, beaten

Melt the butter, chocolate, cream and sugar together in a medium heat microwave for 3-4 minutes. Stir well and add the eggs, beating the mixture as you go.

Pour into a 28cm greased and lined cake pan and allow the mixture to level. Scatter raspberries over the top, not so many you can't see the mixture but enough that you can taste them as you eat the gateau. There's no need to push them in as they fall into the mix during baking.

Pre-heat the oven to 175/180°C and bake for about 35 minutes. When it emerges the cake will be a bit wobbly but will firm up on cooling. As it cools further it will collapse a little into the pan but don't worry about that.

This cake is intensely rich and thin slices would be better to start with.
You can always come back for more

HOT BUTTER SHORTBREAD PASTRY CASE OR TARTLETS

Makes one 28cm tart case or 8-10 tartlets

50g sugar
125g butter
175g plain flour

Pre-heat the oven to 140°C.

Melt the sugar along with the butter in a bowl then stir in the plain flour. Keep stirring until it forms a ball, then let it cool slightly before pressing the mixture into a loose-bottomed tart case.

Bake in a low oven until lightly golden. This takes 10-15 minutes if you are making one large case, 7-8 minutes for smaller tartlettes.

CHOCOLATE AND SALT CARAMEL TART

Makes 12-14 slices

SALTED CARAMEL SAUCE

200g butter

400g light brown sugar

250g double cream

1 teaspoon of maldon salt

TRUFFLE

450g dark chocolate (53% - 60% cocoa)
 broken into pieces

450g double cream

For this tart I spread a thin layer of salted caramel sauce over the base of a 28cm tart case then put it in the freezer. (See previous page for tart case recipe).

When the warm chocolate truffle hits the frozen caramel it starts to set, keeping the two elements separate.

To make the salted caramel sauce, melt the butter in a heavy-based pan over a low to medium heat. Add in the brown sugar to the melted butter and stir well.

Let it simmer away for a 4-5 minutes, stirring occasionally. Remove from the heat and pour in the double cream but be careful as it may foam up. Stir well and add a teaspoon of maldon salt.

Leave to cool a little then pour enough caramel into the tart case to coat the bottom reasonably thickly and pop it in the freezer for at least 1 hour. You can actually leave it in the freezer for up to a week. Excess caramel can be kept in the fridge for up to 4 weeks. It may go grainy on cooling but liquifies when you reheat it.

For the truffle, put the chocolate into a bowl that is big enough to hold the cream as well.

Meanwhile, put the cream in a pan and bring it to the boil. As it starts to rise up the side of the pan, remove it from the heat and pour directly on to the chocolate. Stir slowly, going one way only.

After 1-2 minutes you will start to see the two come together into a beautiful glossy mass (a ganache). Remove the tart base from the freezer and carefully pour over the truffle. Leave to set in a cool place (though not the fridge) for at least 12 hours.

Variation: GANDOLFI CARAMEL SHORTBREAD

To make it feel as if you are having a slice in the Café, press the hot butter pastry mix into a 23x23cm tin and bake for 10-15 minutes in a low oven.

Proceed as for the chocolate tart, maybe using a little more caramel.

BEST TREACLE TART

Makes 12-14 slices

450g golden syrup

125g fresh breadcrumbs

90g ground almonds

2 medium eggs

150ml double cream

2 tablespoons lemon juice

This is the quickest and most delicious treacle tart and is wonderful hot or cold. Begin by making a 28cm hot butter pastry case (see page 163).

Put all the ingredients in a food processor and pulse until everything is amalgamated.

Keep the pre-baked tart case in its tin and pour in the syrup mix. Bake in a pre-heated oven at 175°C for 25-30 minutes.

LEMON TART

Makes 12-14 slices

zest and juice of 2 large lemons

250g caster sugar

200ml double cream

6 eggs

jar good lemon curd

Pre-heat the oven to 140°C. You will also need a 28cm pre-baked hot butter pastry case (see page 163).

The filling for this tart is best made the day before and left to settle in the fridge. Beat together the eggs and sugar, then stir in the cream followed by the lemon juice and zest.

Keeping the case in its tin, pour in the lemon mixture while it is sitting on the middle shelf of the oven. This is simply because it's impossible to move a full tart into the oven without spilling it.

Bake in the oven for approximately 25 minutes. When you remove it from the oven it should not move when you give it a gentle shake. The top will look a bit bubbly and brown in places but don't worry, the inside is smooth as silk.

Remove from the oven and leave to cool. As soon as it is cold, dollop on a few tablespoons of lemon curd and spread gently over the top in a thin layer. This not only saves the tart from cracking, which it is inclined to do, but makes it taste even more wonderful.

FRUIT AND NUT BREAD

Makes 12-14 slices

100g plain flour

1 teaspoon bicarbonate of soda

1 teaspoon baking powder

1 teaspoon salt

145g soft brown sugar

150g dried apricots – cut into 1/3rds

300g dried fruits

280g walnut or pecan halves

3 eggs beaten

Whisk the flour, bicarbonate, baking powder and salt together in a large bowl to make them combine. Then stir in the sugar, add all the dried fruit and nuts and mix together with your hands.

Add the beaten eggs and mix thoroughly with either a rubber spatula or your hands, which will probably make a much better job of it.

Pre-heat the oven to 160°C. Grease and line two 20x10cm loaf tins – the sides as well as it makes it easier to remove the loaves from the tins. Divide the mix between the tins and put both of them on a low shelf in the oven and bake for 30-40 minutes.

When you take them out the tops will be golden brown and the egg and flour mix will be set on the fruit and nuts. Leave to cool in the pan.

It looks jewel-like when cut and is sensational served with cheese or just nibbled on its own. Serve sliced very thinly though.

BANANA AND PECAN LOAF

Makes 12-14 slices

225g self raising flour

1 teaspoon baking powder

100g butter

50g pecan nuts

175g light muscovado sugar

450g ripe bananas, weighed with their skins on

2 eggs

juice of 1 lemon

Put the flour and pecans into the bowl of a food processor and blitz for 15 seconds to grind the pecans. Add the baking powder, sugar and butter and pulse until the mixture looks like breadcrumbs. Tip into a large mixing bowl.

Peel the bananas and break up into the food processor bowl. Break in the eggs and blitz again until you have a relatively smooth puree. Scrape the banana and egg onto the flour and pecan mix and beat well.

Pre-heat the oven to 175°C. Scrape the batter into a 28x10cm loaf tin that has been greased and lined and bake for 35-40 minutes, or until well risen. Let it cool in the tin.

While the cake is still warm, mix together the lemon juice with 2 or 3 tablespoons of icing sugar. Make holes in the top of the cake with a skewer and pour or brush over the lemon and sugar. Let it soak into the cake and allow the whole lot to cool in the pan.

CUPCAKES

Makes 12-16 cakes

250g soft butter

250g self-raising flour

250g sugar

4 eggs

40ml milk

1 tablespoon vanilla extract

Preheat the oven to 180°C and put paper cake cases into a muffin tray.

Put all the ingredients together in a food processor and blitz it for 30 seconds. You may need to scrape down the bowl and blitz again for another 10 seconds.

You can also mix everything together with a hand-held electric whisk. For this, spoon equal amounts into the cupcake cases until they are three-quarters full.

Put them them in the oven for about 20 minutes. Check after 15 minutes and turn the tray if they are browning too quickly on one side.

Leave them to cool in the muffin tray for no longer than 10 minutes before lifting them out and placing them on a rack to cool completely. Decorate with vanilla bean frosting. For the recipe see page 178.

Variations:

CHOCOLATE CUPCAKES

Reduce the self-raising flour to 225g, add 50g of cocoa powder to the flour and proceed as above. Top with chocolate truffle or raspberry frosting. For the recipe see page 178.

WALNUT OR PISTACHIO CUPCAKES

Reduce the flour to 200g, add 100g walnuts or pistachios and process for 20 seconds before you add in the rest of the ingredients.

If you are making pistachio cupcakes, omit the vanilla and add a few drops of rose oil. If you are feeling very fanciful you can bury a piece of rose Turkish delight in each cake before you bake them.

Use coffee frosting for the walnut ones and rose for the pistachio. For the recipe see page 178.

BROWN SUGAR CUPCAKES

This one is pretty obvious too. Just change the sugar to soft brown and, for an even deeper taste, use light muscovado. Just remember to sieve it well before use.

Top with burnt butter frosting. For the recipe see page 178.

FROSTING

Covers 12-15 cakes

500g icing sugar	1 teaspoon vanilla bean paste
125g butter	pinch of salt

Put everything in a food processor and blitz for 30 seconds. Scrape down the side of the bowl and blitz again for 10 seconds. Scrape out into a bowl and chill for about 15 minutes. Any excess can be kept in the fridge for two weeks and you can also freeze it for up to three months.

Variations:

TRUFFLE FROSTING

Make some chocolate truffle (see pages 164-165) and let it set. Add 100g into the food processor mix with the rest of the ingredients but you will need to chill it a little longer.

RASPBERRY FROSTING

Puree 150g raspberries. Push them through a sieve to remove the pips. Substitute the raspberry for the milk and omit the vanilla.

COFFEE FROSTING

Use a cold espresso and make up to 75g, adding water if needed. Omit the vanilla.

ROSE FROSTING

Colour the frosting with a tiny drop of pink food colouring and add a few drops of rose oil. Omit the vanilla.

BURNT BUTTER FROSTING

Put 200g butter in a pan and simmer it gently over a low heat until it turns a light brown, nutty colour. Pour through a fine strainer and discard the residue. Allow the clarified butter to set. Weigh out 125g and use instead of the fresh butter.

TEA CUP TRIFLES

There are no ingredients here, it is totally up to you what you use.

Prepare one teacup and saucer for each guest. Break up some plain cake or Italian sponge fingers in the bottom of each cup. Pour over some liqueur then scatter over some fruit.

Fill the cups two-thirds full with custard and leave to set in a cool place. When you are ready, serve them topped with whipped cream and flaked almonds.

You can tweak the recipe to produce lemon and grape trifles by adding Limoncello liqueur and green grapes or Black Forest by adding in kirsch or raspberry liqueur and topping with cherries or raspberries.

I also like to add Turkish delight for an extra sweet sensation.

AFFOGATO

The easiest and most elegant dessert.

You will need a bowl for each person, although tea cups are also great for this.

Put 2 scoops of very cold vanilla bean ice cream into each bowl and place them in the freezer. When you are ready to serve get a cup of very hot espresso for each person ready with a shot glass of your favourite liqueur next to it.

Place bowls or cups of ice cream on four dinner plates along with the shot glass of liqueur and, at the last minute, give each person a small cup of the very hot espresso. Pour the coffee, then the liqueur over the ice-cream. Heaven.

APPLE BROWN BETTY

Serves 4-6

FOR TOPPING

50g butter

150g fresh breadcrumbs

50g brown sugar

2 teaspoons ground cinnamon

1 teaspoon mixed spice

FOR THE APPLE

1.6kg bramley apples, peeled, cored and roughly chopped

150g sugar

25g butter

Heat the butter in a shallow heavy-based pan. Add the breadcrumbs and stir continuously over a medium-high heat as they become crisp. When they have turned golden, remove them from the heat and stir in the sugar and spices. Allow them to cool.

Place the apples in a heavy-based, non-reactive pan with a splash of water and sugar. Heat gently, cover with a lid and stir occasionally. A smooth puree with a few lumps will result after 10-15 minutes. Remove from the heat, stir in the butter and taste for sweetness.

Serve the warm apple in warm bowls sprinkled with a generous amount of crumbs and lots of whipped cream or crème fraîche.

BREAD PUDDING

Serves 4-6

200g stale brown or wholemeal bread

2-3 teaspoons mixed spice

200ml dark ale (or strong black tea)

75g soft dark brown sugar

50g melted butter

1 large egg

150g currants

25g plain flour

1/2 teaspoon baking powder

caster sugar

Butter the base of a 15cm square cake tin and line with baking paper. Cut the bread into cubes and place in a bowl with the spice.

Warm the ale (or tea) and pour over the bread. Stir, leave to soak for 30 minutes, then scrunch with your fingers into a rough paste. Stir in the sugar, butter and egg, then the currants.

Sift in the flour and baking powder and stir well. Spoon into the prepared tin and smooth the top.

Preheat the oven to 180C. Bake the pudding for 25 minutes, until it is slightly puffed and crisp on top. Remove, dash a spoonful of caster sugar over the top and leave to cool before cutting into squares or fingers.

Index

Acknowledgements

"To the many chefs and staff throughout the years who have given their knowledge and shared their secrets to make the Cafe what it is today. Also, a special thanks to my great friend and inspiration Sam Gardiner."

www.cafegandolfi.co.uk